Headline Series

No. 272   **FOREIGN POLICY ASSOCIATION** $3.00

Third World Radical Regimes
U.S. Policy Under Carter and Reagan
by Anthony Lake

Cover by Hersch Wartik   January/February 1985

The Author

ANTHONY LAKE is professor of international rela-
tions at Mount Holyoke College. He was director
of policy planning in the State Department during
the Carter Administration. He is the author of
*The "Tar Baby" Option: American Policy
Toward Southern Rhodesia;* contributing editor of
The Legacy of Vietnam; and a coauthor of *Our
Own Worst Enemy: The Unmaking of American
Foreign Policy.*

The Foreign Policy Association

The Foreign Policy Association is a private, nonprofit, nonpartisan educational
organization. Its purpose is to stimulate wider interest and more effective
participation in, and greater understanding of, world affairs among American
citizens. Among its activities is the continuous publication, dating from 1935, of
the HEADLINE SERIES. The author is responsible for factual accuracy and for the
views expressed. FPA itself takes no position on issues of U.S. foreign policy.

HEADLINE SERIES (ISSN 0017-8780) is published five times a year, January, March,
May, September and November, by the Foreign Policy Association, Inc., 205
Lexington Ave., New York, N.Y. 10016. Chairman, Leonard H. Marks; President,
Archie E. Albright; Editor, Nancy L. Hoepli; Senior Editor, Ann R. Monjo; Assistant
Editor, K. M. Rohan. Subscription rates, $12.00 for 5 issues; $20.00 for 10 issues;
$28.00 for 15 issues. Single copy price $3.00. Discount 25% on 10 to 99 copies; 30% on
100 to 499; 35% on 500 to 999; 40% on 1,000 or more. Payment must accompany order
for $6 or less. Second-class postage paid at New York, N.Y. POSTMASTER: Send
address changes to HEADLINE SERIES, Foreign Policy Association, 205 Lexington
Ave., New York, N.Y. 10016. Copyright 1985 by Foreign Policy Association, Inc.
Composed and printed at Science Press, Ephrata, Pa.

Library of Congress Catalog Card No. 85-81057
ISBN 0-87124-099-8

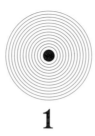

1

Introduction

What do Nicaragua, Afghanistan, Vietnam, South Africa, Angola, Mozambique, Libya and Iran have in common? Each emerges sporadically in the headlines in threatening and puzzling ways. And all can be characterized as "radical regimes."

There are numerous definitions of a radical regime, but a common thread runs through them: Radical regimes show a consistent immoderation in their behavior. For most, this means that their actions regularly and grossly violate those principles of international and national behavior enshrined (if all too inconsistently observed) in the United Nations Charter and the Universal Declaration of Human Rights. In essence, such regimes either

This book is based on a chapter by Anthony Lake in U.S. Foreign Policy and the Third World: Agenda 1985–86, *edited by John W. Sewell, Richard E. Feinberg, and Valeriana Kallab, and published by the Overseas Development Council, Washington, D.C., 1985.*

seek rapid change in the existing order (abroad or at home) or use radical means to preserve that order within their societies.

The immoderation can take many forms. The regimes may be radical in policies domestic but not foreign, or vice versa. They may be of the left (Vietnam) or of the right (Iran), or of both in bewildering mixture (Libya); they may be radical in their principles, in their actions, or in both. They may be hostile to the United States (in many cases) or prefer not to be (South Africa, Angola). They may or may not be "radical" in what was once the prime American definition of foreign radicalism: disrespect for U.S. property.

All radical regimes, however, have one characteristic in common. They are the objects of suspicion in American eyes and of attack in U.S. political rhetoric. In many cases, these regimes came to power through the overthrow of a pro-American government whose own venality and incompetence could not be offset by U.S. protection. In just about all cases, U.S. policymakers—of all Administrations—have failed to deal effectively with radical regimes. Indeed, from Korea to Cuba to Vietnam to Iran and now to Nicaragua, these regimes have, in one way or another, posed some of the most damaging challenges to the United States.

The failures have been conceptual as well as practical. Indeed, beyond noting sporadic efforts to punish or remove such regimes throughout most of this century, it is hard to describe a coherent, much less a consistent, U.S. policy approach to them. During the past eight years, however, two successive Administrations have come to office espousing the two chief and competing U.S. views of how to deal with radical regimes in the Third World. This provides an opportunity to assess their practice of what they professed, bearing in mind two cautions. First, four years is not enough time, the world being what it is, to test conclusively almost any foreign policy proposition. Second, constrained by pragmatic impulses and sometimes by domestic politics, neither the Carter nor the Reagan Administration always pursued the theoretical approaches it espoused.

Nonetheless, a review of U.S. relations with six radical regimes over the past eight years offers a number of lessons about the efficacy of seeking to change the domestic behavior of such a regime or even to change the regime itself, about moderating its foreign policies, about the value of both "carrots and sticks" as instruments of U.S. leverage, about "bleeding" a radical state—that is, draining its human and natural resources—as a lesson for other radicals, and about the ways in which U.S. domestic politics impel and constrain Washington's international policies.

Conflicting Concepts

The two predominant strains in American thinking about this issue go by many names: conservative or liberal, globalist or regionalist, or—more invidiously—accommodative or aggressive. Most policymakers, having once tried to come to grips with the issue, stray from pursuing one or the other course. But even when not pursued as doctrine, the two schools of thought represent clearly distinct predispositions that have shaped mainstream political debates on the issue for the last generation.

There has been little disagreement over basic U.S. interests. Both camps believe that radical regimes tend to pose threats beyond their borders and to the political rights of their own citizens. Both are in favor of limiting Soviet influence in the Third World. Both say they prefer democratic, pluralistic systems and societies. Indeed, these numerous shared assumptions lead others, who believe that economic and social progress can be made only through revolutionary change and the radical restructuring of Third World societies, to lump the two mainstream schools together before dismissing them both.

The disagreements between liberals and conservatives concern methods and priorities. But these are not mere tactical debates. They reflect profound differences over the nature of Third World radical regimes, the severity of the threat such governments pose to U.S. interests, the extent of and reasons for their ties to the Soviet Union, the limits to U.S. influence, and the legitimacy of various means of dealing with these regimes. Much of the difference concerns whether the United States is primarily interested in the competition with the Soviet Union in the Third World, or in the Third World itself.

If you hear it said that radical regimes in the Third World generally are not really Marxist—and even if they are, the United States can work with them on many issues—you will probably also hear that such regimes tend to be highly nationalistic and can thus be weaned from the Soviet Union. In this "regionalist" view, which emphasizes American interests in the region itself rather than focusing, as would a "globalist," on the larger struggle with the Soviet Union, the problems of the Third World tend to be particularistic; a radical regime is thus not necessarily the spearhead of a Soviet thrust into the Southern Hemisphere. Revolution can seldom be exported by radical regimes; it can only be supported by them. It is best to focus not on the wickedness of the radical regime but on the social and economic inequities of its neighbors that create those revolutionary possibilities. According to this view, since most radical regimes seek economic ties with the West, they may be induced to trade in their Mao jackets for pinstripe suits. Therefore, from this perspective, the United States should pursue a path of "constructive engagement" with radical regimes, using economic aid and trade not only to moderate their international behavior but also to promote pluralism and even a little more respect for human rights within their borders—except in the case of South Africa. (Liberals and conservatives share an ideological inconsistency when it comes to South Africa. The negative connotations of the term "constructive engagement" for a liberal, when applied to relations with the South Africans, are precisely the connotations it would have in the mind of a conservative when applied to a leftist regime.) Military pressure, economic sanctions, or harsh words—except, again, in the case of South Africa—tend only to drive these regimes into a defensive shell or into the arms of the Soviets.

Indeed, in this view, the radicalism of such regimes may reflect a failure of the United States to provide sympathy and even support in the early stages of the regimes' existence. Where such governments are actively engaged in conflicts beyond their borders, military aid to their opponents may be appropriate, but the

6

United States should also pursue active diplomatic efforts to resolve the conflicts themselves. Thus, Cuba's Fidel Castro became a Marxist largely because he was spurned by the United States. Yes, he probably still would have been a radical—but not a Soviet client, and not the enemy of the United States. U.S. sanctions drove him further into his dependency on the Soviet Union. He supports revolutionary change in the Western Hemisphere but cannot create it. The United States still can work with him—not only on bilateral issues but also on resolving the conflicts of Central America and even Africa. He pursues a foreign policy that is occasionally independent of Soviet strictures, when this serves Cuban interests; he would like to be still more independent.

If, on the other hand, you hear someone speak of Third World radicalism as synonymous with Marxism, you will almost certainly hear as well that the spread of radicalism in the Third World has a clear pattern and at the center is the Soviet Union. Revolution can be and is exported. The existence of radical regimes thus poses a severe threat to U.S. interests. It is best not only to oppose such efforts by shoring up threatened neighbors but to "go to the source." And radical regimes, by their very nature, are both unrelentingly hostile to the United States and unsusceptible to liberalizing reform through economic ties to the West. According to this view, the United States should pursue a policy of active opposition to radical regimes. Constructive engagement (leaving South Africa aside) only strengthens these regimes and offers them legitimacy. They cannot be reformed; the United States should therefore work for their removal. Instead of offering economic blandishments, the United States should look to economic and other pressures to deter their foreign adventures and even to defeat them at home as well. Thus, Cuba's Castro became a Soviet client not because of U.S. failure to woo him, but because of a failure to prevent the consolidation of his Marxist state before it had become strengthened by Soviet aid and arms. What allows him to act in a hostile manner is not his lack of love for the United States, but his lack of fear of Washington's displeasure.

In this debate, one also hears, sometimes only implicitly, an argument about values—about the legitimacy of certain tactics. At what point, in adopting the tactics of the enemy, does one defeat one's own purpose? Is it legitimate to destabilize a regime because it seeks to destabilize others? to oppose a revolution while it is still popular because it opposes democratic values? to use terrorist tactics against terrorists? to act in an undemocratic fashion in the making of one's own policies for the sake of acting more assertively in defending democracy abroad? to contravene international law in acting unilaterally against those believed to be undermining it?

Questions concerning the nature of Third World radicalism and values underlying how the United States deals with it can and should be answered by analyzing specific cases and by philosophical inquiry (although the latter seldom gets further than the ambiguities illuminated in the soul-searching of John Le Carré's George Smiley). The approaches of the two camps can also be tested, in at least a limited way, by taking as objective as possible a look at how effectively each camp has been able to apply its views over the past eight years. Have radical regimes responded with more-moderate foreign or domestic policies to U.S. efforts at positive economic and political engagement? to U.S. threats or use of force? Do regional strategies focusing on conflict resolution fare as well as, or better than, concentration on support for friends and opposition to the radical state?

These questions about means are tied to judgments about the practicality of possible U.S. objectives in such situations. Can either approach work effectively to moderate the external behavior of radical regimes? Can the United States also change the domestic policies of radical governments, or remove them altogether? Are these objectives mutually reinforcing or antithetical in practice? Alternatively, should the United States simply seek to make life harder for radical regimes, at home and abroad, as an object lesson for others about the costs of radical behavior?

Putting Theory into Practice

The classic case is that of the People's Republic of China (PRC), which was for so long treated in U.S. policy circles as a nonstate. For more than two decades after the victory in 1949 of Mao Zedong and his followers and the retreat of the defeated Nationalist Chinese to Taiwan, the United States sought the international isolation of the Communist regime. In 1972, the dramatic visit of President Richard M. Nixon to China reversed this policy; the new U.S. approach of building more-friendly ties to the PRC was based on the premise that such ties would both promote peace in Asia and prove advantageous in the competition with the Soviet Union.

The futility of U.S. efforts at ostracizing the Communist Chinese leads liberals to claim that they were right in opposing the U.S. China policy; but conservatives may argue that without those years of U.S. ostracism, Chinese internal and external policies would never have evolved to the point where normalization of relations could be considered. Some, indeed, believe that point has not yet been reached. In any case, China presents less-interesting contrasts between the approaches of the last two Administrations than the cases reviewed below. Although Ronald Reagan came to office a strong supporter of the Chinese Nationalists and a skeptic about President Jimmy Carter's establishment of formal diplomatic relations with Beijing, his subsequent policy of seeking to build ever-closer relationships with the PRC between 1982 and 1985 was remarkably similar to that of his three immediate predecessors.

It is more instructive to review the recent histories of six other cases: Nicaragua, Afghanistan, Indochina, southern Africa, Libya and Iran. In all of these cases, the policy approach of each Administration can be tested by the results it achieved. The six regimes involved fall within the loose definition of radical suggested earlier. They differ greatly from one another in character and the challenges they pose, and in the past eight years, they have been the objects of contrasting U.S. approaches.

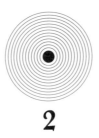

2

The Carter Approach

Of the three objectives the United States might pursue—moderating a radical regime's behavior, removing the regime, or bleeding it as a warning to others—the Carter Administration concentrated almost solely on the first. The primary focus was on seeking to influence the external policies of radical regimes: to gain their cooperation on regional diplomatic issues, to make progress on economic and other bilateral issues, and to weaken their ties to the Soviet Union. Although espousing human rights and criticizing their violation by these regimes, the Carter Administration in most cases did not make the domestic policies of such governments the touchstone for its approach. At least initially, the Administration sought to influence their external behavior through diplomatic and economic blandishments. Force or the threat of force was seldom employed.

Nicaragua

On July 17, 1979, the autocratic government of President Anastasio Somoza Debayle was overthrown. Somoza fled the country and within two days the Sandinista National Liberation

A.G. Smith

Front (named for a Nicaraguan revolutionary who was killed in 1934) took power. The opposition to Somoza's rule had included a wide range of groups in Nicaragua; the Sandinistas, however, had led the military insurgency and now dominated the junta which ruled in Managua.

After failing to prevent a Sandinista victory either by gaining reform of the Somoza regime or, at the last moment, by stitching together international efforts at a moderate resolution of the fighting, the Carter Administration concentrated on gaining leverage with the new regime, seeking to strengthen the more moderate voices within the government and to encourage pluralism in Nicaraguan society as a whole. A $75 million aid program was instituted, after frustrating delays by Congress. The program had the following aims: (a) to allow the United States to compete on the ground with the Soviets and the Cubans, who were sending a small number of military advisers and thousands of civilian teachers, medical workers and the like; (b) to strengthen the position of the middle class, which had provided much support for the Sandinistas but might also have been an important force for economic and political diversity under their rule; and (c) to encourage moderation in Nicaraguan foreign policy, especially with regard to El Salvador, where a growing insurgency against a U.S.-backed government would obviously have the Sandinistas' sympathy if not active support. Seeking either to overthrow the victorious new Sandinista government or to sever completely the long-standing ties between its leaders and their friends in Cuba seemed unrealistic.

Despite evidence that modest amounts of arms were flowing from Nicaragua to the rebels in El Salvador, President Carter in September 1980 provided Congress with the required certification that Nicaragua was eligible for continued U.S. aid since it was not exporting violence to its neighbors. The Nicaraguan government had assured him that any arms that crossed the country's borders were carried by smugglers whose actions contravened Nicaraguan policy. The concern in Washington was that a denial of aid would lead to less rather than more restraint by the Sandinistas with regard to El Salvador and would damage the prospects for some degree of pluralism in a still evolving Nicaraguan political and economic system.

In November and December 1980, however, U.S. intelligence agencies reportedly found evidence of a significant increase in the arms flow to El Salvador and of Sandinista involvement in the smuggling operation. In its last month in office, the Carter Administration suspended—but did not cancel—the aid program, one fifth of which had not yet been provided. Those are the facts; interpretations vary widely. Some argue that the Carter approach was a success. The Sandinistas were interested in U.S. and other Western economic ties and as a result acted only within careful limits in expressing their support for the revolution in El Salvador. But the November 1980 U.S. presidential election led the Sandinistas to conclude that the hard line which Reagan would almost certainly follow when he took office called for preemptive action of their own. They therefore gave more aid to the Salvadoran rebels in preparation for the rebels' January 1981 offensive (which failed, in the event, to achieve the victory the rebels had predicted).

Others interpret the same facts very differently. Increased Sandinista aid to revolutionaries in El Salvador was inevitable; its growth was a function of events in El Salvador and U.S. complacency. The Carter Administration's efforts to improve relations with Castro only encouraged Cuban meddling in both Nicaragua and El Salvador.

Without better knowledge of the policy debates that went on within both Nicaragua and Cuba, it is hard to resolve the difference in the two interpretations. Score it as a <u>possible</u>, and in any case <u>limited</u>, success for the liberal approach. Arms flows <u>were</u> restrained until Carter's defeat. The Sandinista government <u>was</u> clearly prepared to pursue accommodation with Washington on issues beyond Nicaragua's borders. At the same time, the degree to which U.S. aid and diplomacy were encouraging economic, social and political pluralism is ambiguous. It is clear that human rights within Nicaragua fared worse in later years. It is also evident that, within the United States, the Carter approach to this issue was not well received by voters in the 1980 election. Reagan and his supporters used Nicaragua in the campaign, charging that the Sandinista success, like the fall of the shah in Iran, was a sign of Carter's "weakness."

Afghanistan

To a far more limited degree, the same approach was pursued by the Carter Administration with regard to Afghanistan, from the time of the establishment of a Marxist regime in April 1978 until the Soviet occupation of the country in December 1979.

Great-power competition over Afghanistan has a long history. Throughout much of the 19th century, Afghanistan was one of the most important playing fields for the "great game": the struggle between the British and Russians for influence and control throughout the lands along Russia's central southern border. Just as the British feared that Russian control of Afghanistan would pose a threat to their colony, India, so American concerns, 100 years later, centered on the threat that Soviet domination of Afghanistan might pose to friendly governments in Pakistan, on Afghanistan's eastern border, and in the Persian Gulf area, to the south and west.

When Afghan President Mohammad Daud Khan was killed in a military coup on April 27, 1978, and his Marxist successor, Nur Mohammad Taraki, proclaimed the Democratic Republic of Afghanistan, it was clear that Taraki would move Afghanistan away from its traditional balancing act between East and West. And indeed, in December 1978, Taraki went to Moscow to sign a 20-year cooperation treaty with the Soviet Union.

The question for Washington was how best to limit the damage. For almost a year, a policy of active engagement was pursued in the hope that the new regime would act more like "national Communists" than like Soviet clients. Existing economic aid programs continued. U.S. Ambassador Adolph Dubs met frequently with the foreign minister, and there were signs the latter was receptive to maintaining some ties to the West. But in February 1979, Ambassador Dubs was murdered in Kabul, the Afghan capital. Officials in Washington were dissatisfied, to put it mildly, with the way Afghan and Soviet officials performed during the incident, and the period of wooing the Afghan leaders came to an end. Dubs was not replaced by a new ambassador, for understandable reasons. Human-rights abuses and growing Soviet influence were denounced in official statements, and after an April 1979 policy review in Washington, U.S. sympathy for a burgeoning insurgency, organized by Afghan tribal and Muslim leaders, deepened. Nonetheless, statements from Washington continued to express an American desire for "normal and friendly relations," and a chargé d'affaires remained in Kabul to represent U.S. interests.

It has been argued that if policies of engagement had been pursued as firmly after February 1979 as before, President Taraki—or, more likely, his successor, Hafizullah Amin—might have become, if not fiercely independent of Moscow like Yugoslavia's Marshal Tito, then at least as unpredictable an ally of the Soviets as Rumania's Nicolae Ceausescu. After all, in December

1979, the Soviets participated in the bloody overthrow and assassination of Amin at least in part because of his strong streak of independence. Why could Washington not have capitalized more effectively on this?

As with Nicaragua, this is a hard thesis to prove. It is not known how important the U.S. connection was in the calculations made by Afghan leaders. In any case, Washington's options were limited. As the insurgency grew, it became harder for the United States to avoid choosing between the rebels and the Marxist regime. The events of December suggest that a more consistent U.S. policy of engagement might only have led the Soviets to intervene sooner, assuming that Amin's independence as well as domestic unpopularity triggered the Soviet invasion.

by Larry Fogel
Reprinted with permission of *The Washington Post*

Although Nicaragua may have proved an actual, if only partial, success for the liberal approach, Afghanistan provides argument only for a possible but unrealized success. In the event, after the intervention of Soviet military forces at the end of December 1979, both the goals and tactics of the Carter approach shifted. The original policy of containing the damage of the April 1978 revolution became one of active opposition to the regime, through use of economic sanctions and covert but publicly reported aid to the rebels.

Carter did not claim that there could be immediate results either in terms of a Soviet withdrawal or the defeat of the Soviet client regime by the insurgency. But the policy was not one of merely inflicting economic damage on the Communists. Active efforts were made to design and pursue a diplomatic, compromise settlement to the conflict. Such attempts were important to the European allies as they considered whether or not to join in the U.S. sanctions, and also reflected Washington's genuine desire to see the fighting ended. The efforts failed, however, at the conceptual as well as at the practical level. No one could design a political process that might provide the people of Afghanistan some freedom of choice and at the same time prove so attractive to the Soviets that they might be willing to compromise.

Indochina

Upon taking office in 1977, Carter faced the same conceptual choice with regard to Indochina. Should he seek to build bridges to the Marxist regimes in Cambodia (now known as Kampuchea), Laos and Vietnam? Would normalization of diplomatic relations with Vietnam, the most important of the three, weaken the links between Hanoi, Vietnam's capital, and Moscow? Those links were forged during decades of Soviet support for the North Vietnamese military struggle against first the French and then the Americans.

A strategy of competing with the Soviets for influence would be complicated by American memories of the humiliation of the Communist victories in Indochina in 1975, and the remaining bitterness over Hanoi's failure to provide a full accounting of the American servicemen missing in action. But during the first two years of the Carter Administration, U.S. policy toward Vietnam was of a design any regionalist would applaud. Despite its Marxist ideology, efforts would be made at developing a relationship with Hanoi which could serve both American and Vietnamese interests. As future Secretary of State Cyrus R. Vance had written to Carter in a lengthy foreign policy memorandum before the 1976 election, the road to normalization of relations with the Vietnamese government should be explored, since normalization "would give the United States an opportunity to have more influence with a nation which obviously will play an important part in the future development of Southeast Asia." The Vietnamese would welcome normalization, he argued, because it would reduce their dependence on the Soviet Union.

Normalization was explored at a series of meetings with the Vietnamese in 1977 and 1978, but without success. Initial failures came as a result of Vietnamese insistence on U.S. aid—to be called reparations—as a condition of normal relations. By the summer of 1978, the Vietnamese were moving toward greater flexibility, but they found the Carter Administration moving in the opposite direction for a variety of reasons: congressional and political opposition; Vietnamese human-rights abuses and the agony of the "boat people" (the swelling tide of refugees fleeing Vietnam on dangerous and often fatal voyages on the South China Sea); ties between Hanoi and Moscow; and the quickened pace of movement to-

Reprinted with permission of Congressional Quarterly, Inc.

ward normalization of U.S. relations with the PRC, which was itself increasingly hostile to the Vietnamese. The issue was settled by the Vietnamese venture into the Cambodian quagmire in early 1979, when Hanoi's forces drove the genocidal Pol Pot from power after he had launched a series of attacks on Vietnam. The Vietnamese not only saved the Cambodians from the horror of the killing fields; they placed their own client, Heng Samrin, in power, and occupied the country with their troops. As long as Vietnamese troops were occupying neighboring Cambodia, diplomatic relations were deemed by Washington to be impossible in both policy and political terms. Negotiations on such bilateral issues as an accounting of Americans missing in action and the orderly departure of refugees were pursued. A policy of close engagement was not.

Many liberal critics of the Carter Administration's Indochina policy have argued that a great opportunity was needlessly missed. The nationalistic Vietnamese, who have always chafed under dependence on any foreign power, were interested in an American connection as a counterweight to the Soviet Union. Either through incompetence or by giving the Chinese connection unnecessary priority over the Vietnamese, the argument goes, the Carter Administration helped tighten the very ties between Hanoi and Moscow that then became a political barrier to normalization. Indeed, it is argued, progress on the American front might have led the Vietnamese away from an attack on the Cambodians. In short, had the Administration hewed to a purely regionalist approach, the outcome might have been a happier one.

It is true that the Vietnamese were willing to normalize relations, and that this might have reduced their economic dependence on the Soviets. But they were not so eager that they could resist a diplomatic fishing expedition along the way. One senior Vietnamese official involved in the issue recently told some American visitors to Hanoi that, "as diplomats," the Vietnamese "had to try" to get the reparations—that is, to test the limits of American accommodation. Nor should one believe that normalization would have prevented the invasion of Cambodia or precluded increasing Soviet military ties. Those decisions had little to do with Vietnam's relationship with the United States; they had almost everything to do with Vietnam's fear of China and Vietnam's historic designs and disputes in Indochina.

Thus in the Indochina case as in that of Afghanistan, one finds only potential success for the liberal view—in the limited sense that the United States competed with the Soviets and pursued bilateral concerns with Hanoi. The Vietnamese did not want to deal with and diversify their ties to external powers. But neither

Washington nor Hanoi would strike a bargain on terms acceptable to the other.

Southern Africa

The Carter approach did bear fruit in southern Africa. The challenges posed by that region in 1977 formed a tangled web: The white minority regime of Prime Minister Ian D. Smith in Rhodesia (now known as Zimbabwe) was fighting a growing guerrilla insurgency within its borders while defying international economic sanctions. Radical regimes in Angola and Mozambique had recently replaced Portuguese rule. *Apartheid* in South Africa meant that the black majority in that nation lived under totalitarian rule, while the minority enjoyed a "whites only" democracy. And South Africa refused to relinquish its control of the territory which it called South-West Africa and the UN called Namibia.

How could American policy promote solutions to the Rhodesian and Namibian problems while opposing the human-rights abuses of apartheid? The Carter Administration decided on a course that emphasized international cooperation: It would work closely with the British on Rhodesia and the British, French, Germans and Canadians on Namibia, combining their influence to push South Africa to come to terms. It would also seek to work with Angola and Mozambique, together with other black African states in the area, in fashioning the terms of a Rhodesian settlement. And, while making clear its abhorrence of apartheid, it would encourage South Africa to relinquish Namibia and use its influence constructively on Rhodesia by assuring Pretoria, South Africa's administrative capital, that such actions would have a positive effect on future relations between the United States and South Africa.

Policies of engagement with Mozambique, and to a lesser degree with Angola, proved invaluable in British and U.S. efforts to produce settlements in Rhodesia and Namibia. Indeed, it was the successful effort by the government of Mozambique, which persuaded the guerrilla leader Robert Mugabe and his followers to participate in British-held elections, that ended the war and led to independence for Zimbabwe. This followed a series of meetings, over the course of the long Zimbabwe negotiations, between U.S. and Mozambican officials. In 1980, President Carter waived the congressional prohibition of aid to Mozambique and initiated a small program of assistance.

Within Zimbabwe itself, the Western role in bringing about a settlement and the prospects of American and European aid and trade led Mr. Mugabe, who had won the elections overwhelmingly, to establish friendly relations with Washington and other Western capitals while snubbing the Soviets—despite being a self-proclaimed Marxist.

President Carter refused to extend diplomatic recognition, much less aid, to the radical regime in Angola until Cuban troops were withdrawn from that nation, despite State Department recommendations that he offer normalization but not assistance. Neither his National Security Council staff nor the winds of domestic politics favored such a course.

Nonetheless, relations improved, with benefits for both sides. Close consultation with the Angolans regarding the Namibia negotiations helped produce agreement on compromise measures to be offered to South Africa, even if no settlement was reached. Closer ties with the West, an evident Angolan interest, evolved. In the end, the Carter Administration encouraged growing American business interests in Angola and authorized $152.4 million in Export-Import Bank loans and guarantees.

Both liberals and conservatives tend to reverse their prescriptions when it comes to South Africa. While conservatives tend to oppose wooing radicals on the left, they often believe that constructive engagement with South Africa (and other authoritarian regimes on the right) can moderate their behavior. Liberals who call for efforts at improved relations with Hanoi or Managua also tend to argue that only strong pressures against South Africa can have any effect. Carter did take a sterner line with Pretoria than any previous American President, informing the South Africans that a failure to make progress toward ending apartheid would lead to a deterioration in relations with the United States.

A.G. Smith

But this message was tempered by the offer of rewards for good behavior on Zimbabwe and Namibia.

The Carter approach on apartheid met with little success. An arms embargo imposed after the death of black student leader Steven Biko in a South African prison may well have contributed to a decline in the number of South African political prisoners who died in jail. But stern talk and a threatened deterioration in relations with the United States did little to achieve progress toward an end to apartheid.

Thus, in southern Africa, small carrots produced some success in gaining Angolan and Mozambican cooperation on regional issues (although such cooperation was in their interest, in any case); and small sticks produced minor results, but nothing more, within South Africa.

Libya and Iran

In contrast to these examples of partial or potential success of the regionalist approach, the cases of both Libya and Iran convey only failure. The Libyan affair goes back to 1970, when the Nixon Administration essayed a policy of accommodation to the new regime of the mercurial, charismatic, anti-Western Muammar al-Qaddafi. Washington quickly agreed to his request that the Wheelus Air Force Base be evacuated. It is said that Qaddafi was even warned by the Americans of a planned coup d'état. The friendly gestures proved fruitless, however. Qaddafi continued to make life difficult for American businesses operating in Libya, enthusiastically joined in the oil price hikes in the early 1970s and regularly denounced Washington and all its works. By 1972, U.S. representation had been reduced to the level of chargé d'affaires. Relations remained poor in subsequent years. Despite the American interest in Libyan oil and concerns about the potential for foreign troublemaking provided by his oil revenues and his appeal to Islamic revolutionaries beyond his borders, Qaddafi was seen as too unpredictable and too anti-Western to be susceptible to any efforts on the part of the United States at a reasonable relationship.

Libya was thus not given great attention in the first years of the Carter Administration. A Libyan threat against the life of the U.S. ambassador to Egypt was firmly but privately dealt with. The door to an improvement in relations was, at first, carefully left open. But Qaddafi nonetheless regularly denounced American imperialism, and Washington increasingly accused him of supporting terrorism and abusing human rights. An embargo on planes and spare parts was implemented in February 1978. In December 1979, after 66 Americans were taken hostage in Teheran, Iran, a government-backed mob burned the U.S. embassy in Libya's capital, Tripoli. By May of 1980, the last U.S. diplomat had been removed from Libya.

Although the oil trade in Libya remained healthy throughout

this period, by the end of 1980 the United States was represented in Tripoli only by remaining American business people, former Central Intelligence Agency (CIA) officials on unsavory business, and the President's brother, Billy Carter, in his embarrassing visits on personal business. It is hard to judge the Carter policy a failure, since it attempted so little. But the deterioration of U.S.-Libyan relations and Qaddafi's intemperate behavior hardly suggest much in the way of success. The score after a decade: Qaddafi 1, sporadic regionalism in Washington 0.

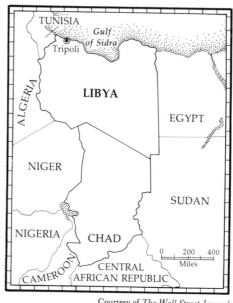

Courtesy of *The Wall Street Journal*

One need not rehearse the sad story of the Carter Administration's efforts to develop some kind of relationship with the regime of the Ayatollah Ruhollah Khomeini in Iran after it came to power in February 1979. The rigidity and narrowness of the religious prism through which the ayatollah viewed the world, and his bitterness at two and one half decades of American support for his enemy, Shah Mohammad Reza Pahlavi, made him extremely suspicious of Washington. The efforts of the Carter Administration to prevent his coming to power, first by seeking to reform the rule of the shah while supporting him, then by backing a moderate alternative to Khomeini, may have loaded the dice against an effort at rapprochement in any case. Washington's persistent efforts to develop some kind of working relationship with Iranian officials in the first months of Khomeini's reign were overwhelmed by the seizure of American

A.G. Smith

diplomatic personnel in Teheran by militants on November 4, 1979—and the refusal of Khomeini's government, for more than 14 frustrating, angry months, to allow their release.

THE RESULTS

President Carter, as well as some of his advisers, was not a pure regionalist. But the thrust of his policies, at least in the early years, was in such a direction. Regionalism as practiced by the Carter Administration achieved some limited success in affecting the international—but not the domestic—behavior of some radical Third World states: Mozambique, Angola and perhaps Nicaragua. It is also at least arguable that, had the Administration pursued such policies in other cases, some further success might have been achieved (in Vietnam and in Afghanistan, for example, although in very limited ways in the first case and with a Soviet invasion still the likely result, in the second). The approach failed in Iran and was barely attempted in Libya. In no case could regionalism be considered a domestic political success for the Administration.

The political difficulties encountered by the Carter policies are not surprising. Liberal regionalist approaches are not only vulnerable to the charge of being "soft on radicalism," but also are inherently difficult to explain in a political context, where the simple argument will always destroy the complex. In contrast, globalist arguments about the Soviet threat can be made consistently in explaining all cases; the anti-Soviet message is a clear one that lends itself to the headline or the 30-second spot on the evening news. Regionalist policies, on the other hand, rely on case-by-case analyses that defy easy generalization and can all too easily seem inconsistent if not incoherent. Indeed, liberals face a fundamental dilemma here: Regionalism calls for heavy reliance on the judgment of regional experts, which is at odds with the liberal instinct in favor of public debate on foreign policy issues.

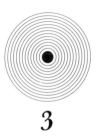

3

The Reagan Approach

Ronald Reagan came to office promising a very different approach. The Carter years, he said, had been a time of retreat and weakness. His own Administration would stand up to foreign challenges, working not only to prevent the emergence of radical regimes (a separate but closely related issue) but requiring those that already existed to behave themselves. During the 1980 campaign, he effectively capitalized on President Carter's problems in Iran, Nicaragua and Afghanistan.

A more "muscular" U.S. approach would not necessarily involve the actual use of force, however. By building up American strength, a Reagan Administration would recapture respect for the United States. This in turn would deter others from challenging U.S. interests. Simply having greater military strength would be enough. In debating President Carter during the campaign, Reagan said, "I don't ever want to see another generation of young Americans bleed their lives into sandy beaches in the Pacific or jungles in Asia or the muddy, bloody battlefields of Europe."

But the radicals of the world, who also tend to be its hard cases, are not so easily cowed, and during his first years in office,

President Reagan found it necessary in almost every case to use force—indirectly and by proxy. One reason for this was that with the muscular stance came an escalation in goals.

In contrast to the Carter emphasis on moderating the behavior of radical regimes, there was now at least an ambiguity about going beyond containment to attempts to remove these regimes from power. Reagan's theoreticians, who saw Moscow and radical ideology as the root of the problem, held little hope for encouraging moderation among radical regimes (except in South Africa). Unwavering, ideological hostility toward the United States called for unwavering, ideological hostility in return. Most notably, in the case of Nicaragua, the Reagan Administration seemed either to believe that containment and "rollback" were on a continuum—pressures applied for the purpose of containment might also lead to destabilization—or to be unable to decide through its internal debates which was the primary goal.

In sum, Reagan's approach (noticeably different from Carter's) demonstrated an ambiguity about rolling back radicalism as well as containing it, a refusal in almost all cases to consider economic inducements, a quicker reliance on force, and a predisposition to let radical regimes and their people be drained in various conflicts.

Nicaragua

The tough new U.S. approach was applied most consistently in the case of Nicaragua. After an initial period of uncertainty, the Reagan Administration pursued two sets of goals: containment, which consisted of halting Nicaraguan aid to the El Salvador rebels, limiting the Nicaraguan military buildup, and inhibiting ties between Managua, Moscow and Havana; and rollback, which implied internal "democratization" and, for some officials, the forced removal of the Sandinista regime. According to press accounts, the internal debates and occasional bureaucratic purges that took place over Central American policy pitted relative moderates (mostly in the State Department and among the military) against hard-liners (mostly in the White House and the

CIA, and among Defense Department civilians). The moderates promoted the first set of goals; the hard-liners insisted on the second set as well and generally prevailed.

The problem with this expansion of goals was twofold. First, no foreign policy will be judged fully successful if its accomplishments fall short of the goals that are set for it. And in Nicaragua, a number of President Reagan's goals seem beyond the reach of his means. Second, the two goals of containment and rollback do not lie on a continuum; efforts at destabilization help persuade a regime that there is no point in agreeing to limit its foreign actions or to moderate its behavior at home. If U.S. hostility is unrelenting, why concede on any point? Why be "contained" if this will not alter Washington's approach? Thus assumptions of hostility on both sides become self-fulfilling.

Pressure against the Sandinistas took a number of forms. At the end of 1981, the President authorized the most thinly veiled covert operation since the CIA-backed Bay of Pigs invasion provided Castro a triumph and President John F. Kennedy a terrible public humiliation in 1961. As it evolved over more than 30 months, the anti-Nicaragua program entailed support for paramilitary operations within as well as beyond Nicaragua and was aimed at economic as well as military targets. In addition, a series of U.S. military exercises in Honduras and off Nicaragua's shores seemed clearly designed to intimidate the Sandinistas. The Administration sought to do further economic damage by opposing loans from the multilateral development banks and discouraging bilateral aid donors.

In regional political councils and in speeches at home, President Reagan and his representatives pursued efforts to isolate the Sandinistas. In Washington's rhetoric, Nicaragua was a "totalitarian dungeon"; the United States would not let it become a "platform for terror and war." Such rhetoric not only reduced U.S. flexibility should the Administration ever have wished to adopt more-moderate policies, but also implied that the ultimate goal of U.S. policy was precisely that held by the hard-liners in the White House and at the CIA: the overthrow of the Sandinistas. And indeed the pattern of operations of the anti-Sandinista

Nicaragua's Daniel Ortega Saavedra addresses a Foreign Policy Association meeting in New York, October 1, 1984.

guerrillas as well as their obvious intentions cast doubt on the Administration's assertions that it did not seek the destabilization of the Nicaraguan regime. The infamous manual developed by CIA consultants for the guerrillas not only encouraged such repellent methods as assassination but also promoted the overthrow of the Nicaraguan government. By June 1985, there was increasing talk among officials in Washington of the possibility of a future invasion of Nicaragua.

Not all of the Reagan Administration's approach was purely punitive, however. Sporadic efforts were made at engaging the Sandinistas in negotiations; the State Department pushed the "efforts" while the hard-liners reportedly preferred the "sporadic." Here, too, U.S. policymakers seemed to see the goals of gaining international moderation and internal change on a continuum. With increasing rigidity, the United States insisted that without "democratization" inside Nicaragua, there could be no agreement on issues between the two nations. By the fall of

1984, diplomatic maneuvering was again increasing. But no progress on substantive issues seemed possible as long as Washington insisted on rearranging internal Nicaraguan affairs— and none was made during the first half of 1985.

When goals seem unattainable, three courses of action are possible. First, the unsatisfactory position may simply be continued. Second, more pressure may be threatened or applied. (But in late 1984 and 1985, increasing threats seemed only to be creating closer ties between Managua and Moscow.) Third, more-moderate goals may be introduced. The experiences of early 1981 and late 1983 suggest that more-modest goals—external containment and agreement to limit the Soviet and Cuban military presence—might have been achievable. During the spring of 1981, the Nicaraguan government seemed to be acting out of fear of the sticks that Reagan had said he would use and out of hope for economic-assistance carrots. The Sandinistas reportedly closed a clandestine radio beaming rebel broadcasts into El Salvador, gave assurances that they would refrain from further aid to the rebels, and actually began to reduce the flow of weapons. This was not enough for Washington, however, and the U.S. aid program was definitively canceled. Talks initiated by the State Department in the summer continued into the fall, but the little progress made was destroyed by increasingly acerbic rhetoric on both sides.

Similarly, in late 1983, U.S. pressures had apparently helped convince the Nicaraguan government to seek a regional settlement along lines proposed by third parties. In January 1983, the leaders of Colombia, Mexico, Panama and Venezuela met on the Panamanian island of Contadora to discuss ways of ending the deepening conflicts in Central America. On September 9, 1983, the "Contadora" countries proposed a 21-point plan, or set of principles. In January 1984, the Nicaraguan government joined other Central American governments in accepting the Contadora "principles for implementation." But Washington's terms had become even more demanding than in 1981, especially with regard to "democratizing" Nicaragua's internal politics. The

Sandinistas considered this a call for their surrender, not a settlement, and the opportunity was lost.

To judge the success of the Reagan approach in its own terms, let us look at the goals listed previously. In the first years containment failed to keep arms flows down to the levels of most of 1980 and early 1981; by 1985, ties to the Soviets and Cubans were stronger than ever; throughout the period the Nicaraguan military buildup continued. It appeared that the U.S. position was only strengthening hard-line views in Managua; Nicaraguan leaders could conclude that any concession on such issues would only encourage Washington in pursuit of its other goal—their destruction.

This is not to argue that the goal of democracy in Nicaragua is an unworthy one. It is to suggest that efforts at forcing the Sandinistas to relinquish power are most unlikely to make them more accommodating on "democratization" or any other issue. Indeed, the partial economic embargo against Nicaragua announced by the Administration in the spring of 1985 could weaken the prospects for democracy by harming the small businesses which provide an important pluralistic element in Nicaraguan society. The sanctions, opposed by the United States' European allies, were most unlikely to force change in the Nicaraguan government's behavior—unless to push it toward greater dependency on the Soviet Union.

Economic damage had been inflicted but there were few signs that the U.S.-supported attacks (through the embargo and through earlier support for guerrilla attacks on commercial targets) had rolled back the Nicaraguan revolution. Although Nicaraguan economic problems detracted from the Sandinistas' popularity, U.S. pressure gave them an explanation and an issue against their adversaries. Although elections were held in the fall of 1984 (perhaps partly in response to international pressure) and some opponents of the regime were allowed to campaign against the Sandinistas, the terms of the election did not satisfy Washington or much of the Nicaraguan opposition, who withdrew from the campaign. Although the anti-Sandinista guerrillas, the so-called contras, seem likely to receive U.S. aid, congressional concerns seem likely to limit it to "nonmilitary" aid distributed by agencies other than the CIA. All in all, not a strong record of success for the Administration's approach.

Libya

The initial approach of the Reagan Administration toward Libya was in some ways very similar to its Nicaraguan policies. Just as Nicaragua was used by Administration spokesmen to dramatize the threat to security in Central America and the difference in approach from that of the Carter years, so Libya and its leader were used to demonstrate both the threat of international terrorism—a major theme of early speeches by Secretary of State Alexander M. Haig Jr. and others—and, again, the contrast with Carter's policies. No more Billy Carter visits to Tripoli; now, Qaddafi would be brought to heel.

Again, a policy of pressure against the offending government was implemented. In May 1981, Libyan diplomats were expelled from the United States following revelations that Libyan students in this country had been victims of Libyan government hit men. Washington announced that it considered travel by Americans to Libya to be hazardous. In August 1981, two Libyan aircraft were shot down in a dogfight over the Gulf of Sidra. A policy review within the Administration considered complete sanctions against Libya.

The Administration apparently intended to pursue containment, rollback and bleeding all at the same time. Military aid to Libya's threatened neighbors—notably Chad, Sudan and Tunisia—would be increased, where needed. Economic sanctions would reduce Qaddafi's ability to make trouble abroad while creating economic difficulties that might imperil his rule at home. Encouragement for Hissene Habré, the anti-Libyan leader of one of the two main factions contending for power in Chad, might help limit Libyan influence there.

But the initial impulse was tempered by a concern for U.S. economic interests. The review culminated in a decision in

Col. Muammar al-Qaddafi reviews a military parade in Tripoli on the 15th anniversary of the Libyan revolution, September 1984.

December 1981 to impose only partial sanctions. A step-by-step approach, it was decided, made more sense both in terms of effectiveness with Qaddafi and, of course, for U.S. business dealings with Libya. The legal complexities encountered by the Carter Administration in pursuing sanctions against Iran were also an inhibiting factor. The decks were cleared for further action, however: After announcing (but never offering evidence) that the Libyans had sent a hit squad to the United States with the President as its target, the Administration asked all Americans to leave Libya. In March 1982, all oil imports from Libya (by then down to less than 1 percent of U.S. consumption) were banned, as were high-technology exports.

Perhaps because Secretary of State George P. Shultz customarily spoke in a lower key than his predecessor, or on account of the Reagan Administration's concern about the damage that

further sanctions might do to U.S. corporations, or because our European allies were most unenthusiastic about economic sanctions, or because Qaddafi moderated his behavior during 1983, or because of a realization that rhetorical or any other kind of attention is what the Quaddafis of the world most crave— whatever the reasons, the focus during most of the period from 1982 to 1985 was more on support for threatened neighbors than on further public pressure against Libya itself. When Libyan troops invaded Chad, the French were urged to respond militarily. American words as well as deeds were surprisingly muted. The "step-by-step" approach to economic sanctions had effectively stopped with the embargo of March 1982.

Did the "toughness" of 1981 and the relative pragmatism from 1982 to 1985 produce results? If so, was it more the muscle or the moderation that did so?

Qaddafi clearly went through a period of relative pragmatism during 1982 and much of 1983. He withdrew the forces that had been occupying much of Chad since late 1980; reportedly put a halt to any targeting of Americans; and stopped attempting to assassinate Libyan dissidents abroad. It may well be that his restraint was caused by fear of Reagan's wrath and the loss of Libyan jets to American firepower over the Gulf of Sidra. But his troop withdrawal from Chad was clearly related to his hopes of currying favor within the Organization of African Unity while maneuvering for its chairmanship. It is not clear that the threat to President Reagan was in fact real. And Qaddafi's campaign against Libyan dissidents was earning him a well-deserved hostility abroad that he apparently did not enjoy.

However, in the summer of 1983, Qaddafi sent forces back into Chad and, in 1984, attacks on Libyan exiles began again. If Qaddafi remained deterred from attacks on Americans, in August the blood of a British policewoman, shot from a window of the Libyan embassy during an anti-Qaddafi demonstration in London, showed that the Libyans had not yet adopted international Marquis of Queensberry Rules. Conservatives would argue that the end to Qaddafi's moderation may have been the result of a diversion of U.S. attention (and warships) to Lebanon during the crises of 1983 and the deployment of U.S. Marines there. Liberals would suggest that it had to do more with events in Chad and with the May 8, 1984, coup attempt inside Libya. Did Qaddafi start to attack his opponents in the preceding months because he had sniffed a plot in the wind? Did he tighten up at home and become less moderate abroad because he believed, whatever the facts of the case, that Americans were plotting his overthrow?

By the spring of 1985, although Qaddafi was pursuing an active diplomacy in the Arab world (including a startling liaison with Morocco and efforts at a rapprochement with Sudan) and encouraging European investors to expand their Libyan operations, he did not seem to be entering a new period of moderation. His promises in 1984 of another military withdrawal from Chad had not been kept. The lid on opposition within Libya remained tightly in place. Allegations in 1984 of Libyan intent to bomb Egypt's Aswan Dam and of complicity in the mining of the Red Sea suggested that Qaddafi's appetite for troublemaking remained large. In mid-December 1984, the Reagan Administration again asked Americans to leave Libya, and in June 1985, it ordered a Libyan diplomat at the UN, accused of plotting against Libyan dissidents in the United States, to leave the country.

With as unpredictable a character as Qaddafi, it is not surprising that the role of threats and rewards in influencing his behavior, or even what his behavior might be, is unclear. One thing does seem clear: A towering ego loves attention, and the modest American rhetoric of 1983-84 seemed better calculated to encourage moderation than the rhetorical bluster of 1981, which probably had only appealed to his vanity.

Iran

The Reagan Administration's approach to the Khomeini regime in Iran was much closer to the quiet of the latter stages of its Libyan policies than the sound and fury of the early campaign against Qaddafi. Iran was of course a major item in Reagan's bill of particulars against Carter during the campaign, and many expected him to use Khomeini as a symbol of the world's evils, much as he used Qaddafi and the Sandinistas. But perhaps Reagan and his advisers had no desire to repeat the Carter mistake of playing up Khomeini even more than his actions warranted. More important, the Administration likely saw that attacking a non-Marxist, indeed an anti-Marxist, regime would only play into the hands of the Soviets. More concerned about the threat to Iran from the Soviets in the north than about the threat posed by Khomeini to friendly Persian Gulf states to his south, the Administration was led by its anti-Soviet preoccupation to a relatively relaxed policy toward an anti-American radical. Paradoxically, ideological calculations produced pragmatic policies.

This is not to say that U.S. attitudes and actions toward Iran were in any way friendly. American policy has tilted somewhat toward Iraq in the Iran-Iraq war, which has dragged on for five years, at appalling human cost, since the initial Iraqi attack in the fall of 1980. The tilt has been limited by Iraq's reported use of chemical warfare, its ties to the Soviets, and the fact that the regime in Iraq almost matches its neighbor in domestic human-rights abuses. After allegations of Iranian complicity in the October 1983 terrorist attack against the Marines in Lebanon, which resulted in the deaths of 241 American servicemen, the President properly added Iran to the list of nations that have "repeatedly provided support for acts of international terrorism." Administration officials also are said to have met quietly with some key Iranian exile leaders.

Yet consider what the Administration might have done. Despite initially toying with the idea, it did not renounce the financial arrangements (concerning transfers of frozen Iranian assets from the United States to Iran, settlement of claims against Iran and the like) made by the Carter Administration in gaining the release of the hostages, and it allowed modest economic intercourse to continue. It did not make a major public issue of Khomeini and the brutality of his regime, although some specific human-rights abuses were criticized. It did react with verbal warnings and enhanced support for friendly Persian Gulf states

**Ayatollah Ruhollah Khomeini about to address followers
in the Holy City of Qom.**

in response to Iranian threats and actual attacks on shipping, but
it avoided direct military involvement. It did not, at least as far as
one can tell, support anti-Khomeini exiles through a covert-action
program. Although it normalized relations with Iraq on November 26, 1984, it did not tilt toward Iraq nearly as far as it might
have or as much as some Arab friends wished it to. And it did not
retaliate against Iran for terrorist attacks against American
personnel in Lebanon, despite the strong suspicion that Iran was
involved. Washington reportedly decided that such retaliation
might only produce further attacks. In the spring of 1985 there
was new talk in Washington of retaliation for Iranian support of
terrorism in Lebanon and elsewhere, but again, no action.

It would be unfair to emphasize that the Reagan policies
toward Iran did not accomplish much; not much could have been
accomplished. The policies were reactive and pragmatic where
pragmatism was called for. Washington, perhaps too easily in

light of the high human cost, accepted the advantages of letting Iran and Iraq have at it. But the way to achieve a diplomatic solution to that conflict was not immediately apparent. In short, it was a situation in which there were more opportunities to make things worse than openings to make them better—and the Reagan Administration, to its credit, showed restraint.

Afghanistan and Indochina

Although Nicaragua and Libya—and Iran in the first days of January 1981—were used to demonstrate differences between the Reagan and Carter approaches, Reagan's policies toward Afghanistan and Indochina, specifically Cambodia, were similar to those of his predecessor. In these two cases, of course, Carter, after attempting policies of diplomatic engagement, had ended up indirectly endorsing the use of force. Indeed, in ending the partial grain embargo against the Soviet Union soon after taking office, Reagan took a somewhat less muscular approach than had his predecessor to one aspect of his Afghanistan policies. Remarkable parallels can be found in the Reagan approaches to Afghanistan and Cambodia. His policies in the two cases were similar in their goals, in their reliance on force, and in their reactive diplomatic stances.

In both cases, the Reagan Administration sought the removal of an offending regime: the Babrak Karmal regime in Afghanistan and that of Heng Samrin, Hanoi's client, in Cambodia. The American position supported self-determination for both peoples—constituting, in effect, a call for the removal of unpopular regimes then in power.

In both cases, the position of working for the removal of a Marxist regime was different in fact and legality from calling for the removal of regimes that had gained power through revolutions that were primarily indigenous, as in Nicaragua. Both regimes had been brought to power and sustained by the military forces of powerful neighbors: the Soviet Union and Vietnam.

In both cases, some form of economic sanctions was pursued against a neighboring aggressor nation, although the sanctions

Afghan President Babrak Karmal holds a news conference in Moscow.

were much stronger against Vietnam, where they hurt U.S. economic interests less.

In both cases, although in different ways, American support was given to rebels fighting against the radical regime—rebels supplied by or based in neighboring countries friendly to the United States (Pakistan and Thailand). Under Reagan, support for the insurgency in Afghanistan was channeled, as under Carter, through a covert CIA program that became public knowledge. Support for the coalition of forces fighting against the Heng Samrin regime in Cambodia reportedly has not involved the U.S. provision of military supplies, although in mid-1985 Representative Stephen J. Solarz (D-N.Y.) was seeking congressional approval of assistance to the non-Communist elements of the resistance forces. But it has involved diplomatic support in various forms, as well as approval of Beijing's provision of military supplies to the rebels.

In both cases, Washington could be accused of political error in its selection of the rebel groups with which it became associated, although its support of forceful resistance to aggression is not widely criticized.

Under Reagan as under Carter, U.S. policy was to support the former regime of Pol Pot as the legitimate claimant to Cambodia's seat in the UN, but to oppose his return to actual power in Cambodia. American sympathies lie with Pol Pot's uneasy allies, Prince Norodom Sihanouk and former premier Son Sann. But by acquiescing so easily to Chinese support of the Pol Pot regime, the United States allowed itself to become associated with one of the most loathsome figures of modern history.

In Afghanistan, Washington reportedly directed its aid to those rebel groups most favored by the Pakistani government. Partly for internal political reasons, the Pakistanis are said to prefer Muslim fundamentalist guerrilla leaders, although their political support within Afghanistan may not be as deep as that of the local chieftains who have traditionally ruled the countryside. In the long run, Islamic fundamentalism also may not be the best trend to encourage from the point of view of U.S. interests. Similarly, in Nicaragua, the support not only of disaffected former Sandinistas but also of former supporters of the unpopular Anastasio Somoza created difficulties both within Nicaragua and among the rebel forces.

In both Afghanistan and Indochina, neither Carter nor Reagan officials held out much hope for military success in any foreseeable future. And in both cases, the Reagan Administration left diplomacy to regional friends. Washington was generally passive, if supportive, as the Pakistanis in the first case, and the Association of Southeast Asian Nations (ASEAN, whose members are Brunei, Indonesia, Malaysia, Philippines, Singapore and Thailand), in the second, offered diplomatic solutions to the conflicts. This made sense in terms of short-run U.S. interests. Relations with regional friends have been strengthened, and the prospects for negotiated settlements in any case are not bright—despite Hanoi's occasional indications that it is ready to negotiate a Cambodian settlement. The entirely proper U.S. insistence on self-determination as part of a solution was inherently unattractive to regimes dependent for their existence on the presence of foreign military forces.

But, in the long run, diplomatic passivity could lead to opportunities for settlement being missed when the participants in the fighting are ready to move to serious talks. In the case of Indochina, the Reagan Administration did well to welcome Hanoi's statements in 1984 about the desirability of a settlement. And progress toward a bilateral agreement on the emigration from Vietnam of thousands of Amerasian children and prisoners held in Vietnamese "reeducation" camps was to be praised. But more could be done to promote a regional peace: It would serve a number of U.S. interests to urge China and the ASEAN nations to remove Pol Pot and his chief lieutenants from the leadership of the Communist Khmer Rouge government which was driven from the capital when the Vietnamese invaded in December 1978. Such a step would not only strengthen the political position of the coalition within Cambodia and in world opinion, but could also improve the prospects for diplomatic progress, since the Vietnamese claim that the major sticking point in any compromise is the possibility of Pol Pot's return.

Southern Africa

The Reagan approach to southern Africa was an exception to the pattern of behavior shown in the other cases. Here, the Administration pursued a policy of diplomatic engagement not only with South Africa but also with its neighbors who had proclaimed Marxist ideologies. U.S. diplomats were very active in pursuing a settlement in Namibia, although with little evident progress, and attempting to improve relations between Pretoria and its neighbors, with apparent results in the achievement of a nonaggression pact between South Africa and Mozambique and a cease-fire between South Africa and Angola along the Namibian border. Indeed, State Department officials argue both that such diplomatic activism is in the U.S. interest and that only the United States is in a position to deal with both sides along the racial fault line in the region.

Diplomatic activism is not the only difference between this case and the others. Although the United States, by taking a neutral position on South Africa's use of force against its neighbors, indirectly applied sticks to those neighbors, it also offered them carrots. After Mozambican and South African leaders signed a nonaggression pact known as the accord of Nkomati in March 1984, the Reagan Administration for the first time submitted a waiver to Congress and announced an economic assistance program for Mozambique, in addition to generous emergency food supplies. At the beginning of 1985, it went further, requesting $1 million from Congress for nonlethal military aid. This was increased to a request for $3 million in such aid for fiscal year 1986, despite opposition by some of its own conservative supporters in the Congress.

The Administration showed remarkably little concern about the ideological makeup of the Angolan and Mozambican governments. Despite these regimes' espousal of radical philosophies, Secretary of State Shultz met with the Angolan Interior Minister in April 1983, and in late 1983 the United States restored relations with Mozambique to the ambassadorial level. To be sure, the Administration was clearly sympathetic to Dr. Jonas Savimbi and his guerrillas in their struggle against the Angolan government, refused recognition of the Angolan government, and wished to see Mozambique join the International Monetary Fund in order to encourage its pragmatic move away from a government-directed economy. But in general, the Administration pursued its diplomacy without letting ideological differences bar professional exchanges of views.

The regional issue on which the Reagan Administration acted in the most ideological manner was the one on which it achieved the least: Namibia. By insisting that Cuban forces be withdrawn from Angola at the same time as any settlement was implemented in Namibia, rather than as its consequence, Reagan greatly complicated an already complex issue and earned the disapproval both of African states and of our European partners in the Namibian negotiations. A settlement remained possible even on those terms, but it had apparently been further delayed by this linkage.

Some would argue that the success of the accords between South Africa and its neighbors was no real success at all. Angolan and Mozambican agreements with South Africa had been forced not so much by U.S. diplomacy as by South African pressure and the devastating effects of regional drought. Furthermore, they argue, the United States had only achieved complicity in the temporary certification of South African dominance of weaker states along its borders. And its policy of constructive engagement with South Africa had, in its softened stand on apartheid, earned the anger of Africans across the continent—as well as the opposition of a growing number of U.S. congressmen of both parties, who were moving in the spring of 1985 toward some form of economic sanctions against South Africa. Indeed, in June 1985, after a series of attacks by South African military forces within Angola and Botswana, and a new round of violence within South Africa, even the Administration expressed its displeasure by ordering the American ambassador in Pretoria back to Washington.

But in his own terms, Reagan's policies in this region had largely succeeded. All but the South Africans had accommodated themselves, at least in part, to U.S. goals. And the Soviets were clearly displeased by what had happened. Indeed, officials in Moscow were telling American visitors that southern Africa had been moved down on their scale of priorities. Ironically, the greatest success had been achieved where the Administration had acted least according to form: by providing carrots while leaving the sticks more or less to others, by pursuing an activist diplomacy, and by dealing with the radicals in a relatively unideological fashion.

Why had such policies been pursued in southern Africa but not in Nicaragua? The answer would seem to lie in propinquity and politics. The farther an issue was from the United States and from its political debates, the easier it was for the pragmatists in the Administration to hold sway.

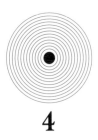

4

Implications for Future Policy

What do the Carter and Reagan experiences in all these cases tell us about the most practical approaches the United States might in the future take toward radical regimes in the Third World? More specifically, which objective—moderation of their external behavior or their removal by bleeding them—has been most nearly achieved? Which tactics—carrots or sticks—have been most effective? Are efforts at their isolation or policies of diplomatic engagement more productive?

These six cases provide clear differences between the Carter and Reagan approaches: Under Reagan, more emphasis has been placed on the removal of offending regimes, a higher tolerance or even encouragement of conflicts that impose costs on radical regimes and their people, a less activist diplomacy, more reliance on the threat or use of force, and less reliance on economic blandishments. And, as seen in his support for the Nicaraguan contras and their methods, Reagan seems to have been less concerned than Carter with the dilemma of how one competes with an ideological opponent in ways that do not contradict U.S. values.

But neither approach has been notably successful. Perhaps the more important lessons to be drawn are found not in a competitive comparison, but by looking for instructive patterns in the experiences of both Administrations. Ten such patterns seem to emerge:

● 1. It is interesting that in no case, in either period, was there any success in removing a radical regime or even significantly affecting its internal behavior. This does not mean that it is impossible, as U.S. involvement in the 1973 overthrow of President Salvador Allende in Chile demonstrated. (The years of political repression and abuse of individual rights under his successor, General Augusto Pinochet Ugarte, hardly provide evidence for the general wisdom of such a goal.) The point is that efforts either to prevent the consolidation of revolutions (in states less vulnerable than Grenada, the small Caribbean island where American military forces removed a brutal radical regime in October 1983) or to induce such regimes to liberalize in their early stages may be more difficult than either globalist or regionalist rhetoric has seemed to imply. The lesson here is clear: The limits of U.S. leverage are narrower than either liberals or conservatives like to believe.

● 2. It may well be that there are opportunities to encourage trends toward pluralism within revolutionary states once they have had full experience with the difficulties of trying to manage their economies through central (and generally inefficient) bureaucracies. It is clear that pragmatic impulses are on the rise in, for example, China, Vietnam, Angola and Mozambique. But in their first years in power, revolutionary regimes may be the least receptive to external efforts to influence their internal policies, perhaps because of the very fragility of the infant institutions they seek to protect and build.

● 3. There were, however, some partial successes, either potential or real, affecting the foreign policies of these regimes: southern Africa in both periods; Nicaragua in 1980 before November and again in 1981; perhaps Libya in 1982-83; and potentially Vietnam during both the Carter and Reagan Administrations.

● 4. However, when the goal of rollback was pursued at the same time as efforts to induce foreign moderation, the former seemed to interfere with the latter. Such was the case in Nicaragua, and perhaps in Libya in May 1984.

● 5. It is not difficult to stand by and allow, or even to encourage, the bleeding of a radical regime in some local conflict—as in the later Carter years and under Reagan with regard to Afghanistan, Nicaragua, Iran and Iraq, and Indochina. In some cases, it is also practical to impose economic costs on such regimes, as a warning to revolutionaries elsewhere. But do such policies truly serve American interests in the long run? The danger to regional friends of becoming involved in such conflicts is very real and also involves dangers to the United States. How far, for example, is Washington prepared to go in helping defend Pakistan from possible Soviet attack, as the Soviet forces in Afghanistan move closer and closer to the Pakistani border (and sometimes, reportedly, beyond it) in their military operations? The economic consequences of such conflicts are not insignificant, as demonstrated by the Iran-Iraq war, which has affected oil exports to the rest of the world. And beyond the issues of U.S. interests is the fundamental issue of morality. Bleeding a radical regime is not an abstract metaphor: It means the blood of Iranian children, of Cambodian or Nicaraguan villagers and soldiers, of other human beings. The political ends of the bleeding must consciously be weighed against the suffering inflicted on a people who may not be responsible for the actions of their government.

This is not to say that in these cases the United States could have produced a diplomatic miracle. It is to argue that inflicting, or being indifferent to, such a situation serves neither American interests nor American ideals.

When it comes to the means employed, the record is mixed.

● 6. The blandishments preferred by liberal theorists have apparently had some limited impact in southern Africa, in Nicaragua in 1980, and in the reported desire for improved relations expressed by Vietnam and, from time to time, by Cuba. As noted, a policy of carrots has also, in some cases, failed.

Members of an Afghan patrol near the Pakistan border.

● 7. Similarly, the sticks wielded by Reagan have sometimes influenced the behavior of radical regimes: in Nicaragua in late 1983 and perhaps in Libya during the period of Qaddafi's moderation in 1982 and early 1983.

● 8. The greatest successes or opportunities came, however, when carrots and sticks were combined: in southern Africa and in Nicaragua in early 1981. Similarly, the success of the Carter Administration in helping the British achieve a settlement of the Rhodesian conflict came through a policy of pressures and promised rewards.

● 9. A policy of diplomatic engagement paid off for both the Carter and Reagan Administrations in the case of southern Africa. Efforts to isolate radical regimes do not seem to have worked, as seen in the cases of Libya (early under Reagan) and Nicaragua, where Washington's economic boycott seems destined primarily to strengthen Sandinista resolve and to hurt private businesses.

● 10. Where there has seemed little possibility of either carrots or sticks inducing significant change in the behavior of a regime (as in Iran or Libya), the low-key policies of 1982-84 served the Reagan Administration better, in both foreign and domestic political terms, than a barrage of hostile rhetoric.

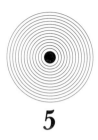

5

Conclusion

Judging by the events of the past eight years, it would seem clear that no single theoretical approach always, or even almost always, works. This does not mean that debating the issue at a broad level of generality is useless, nor that these archetypical approaches have no value. Through such debates, important attention is given to questions about the fundamental goals and values that the United States should be pursuing when facing the challenges posed by Third World revolutions. But it seems clear that whether a nation's goals are primarily global or regional in character, neither regionalist nor globalist doctrine can by itself provide consistently effective policies.

Policies can best be shaped, therefore, by asking questions about each situation rather than by pretending to know the theoretical answers even before the questions are posed. Radical regimes vary widely in their governing structures. It is not surprising that these "different folks" respond to "different strokes." In each case, policymakers would do well to ask questions such as the following: How deeply are U.S. interests involved? What is the nature of the regime in question? Do its decisions reflect internal debate and discussion that might be influenced (as with the Sandinistas) or the private impulses of an individual, like Quaddafi, whose decisionmaking process is not entirely clear? What is the true scope of potential American influence? What do U.S. allies and regional friends think, and what are they prepared to do? If U.S. policy fails, is the exit clear?

The answers to such questions may be very different in each case. This suggests, in turn, that U.S. policy toward radical regimes should be characterized more by flexibility and patience than by doctrinal purity. The difficulty of dealing with such regimes also suggests that there is seldom value to rhetorical holy wars, to promising easy results, and thus to turning policies in these cases into public tests of American foreign policy as a whole. Rhetorical excess in Washington only leads to political embarrassment at home, diplomatic rigidity abroad, and expanded egos for the objects of American diatribes. A Khomeini or a Qaddafi is not shocked or hurt when attacked by Washington; he only knows that the United States understands his importance. A Sandinista is not moved to accommodation; he becomes convinced that accommodation might be a fatal weakness. And in the long run, the American voter is not impressed when results fall short of rhetoric.

But is such pragmatism in Washington really possible? A policy of flexibility and patience depends, finally, on the flexibility and patience of the American public. Radical regimes and their leaders make wonderful targets in domestic political speeches and produce exciting images on the evening news. They easily become major figures in the American mind. It is thus not surprising that from the Bay of Pigs to the Iranian rescue mission, American Presidents have felt impelled by public impatience as well as other concerns toward ill-advised action. Yet, since the Vietnam war, polls have generally shown that while the public wants success (the defeat of these regimes), it must come at little cost to the United States (that is, involve no great losses through intervention, grain embargoes, or other actions).

Both Secretaries of State Henry Kissinger, with his intricate policies of détente, and Cyrus Vance, with his efforts to manage relations in a complicated world through complex American policies, discovered the difficulty of building public support for a sophisticated American stance abroad. Some might therefore turn to the cynical course of sacrificing effectiveness abroad for popularity at home, making policy through simple slogans. Others might despair and turn away from policies of complexity because they can so easily be attacked as policies of incoherence or conciliation. Surely the United States can afford neither course. The first requirement is an understanding that a policy of pragmatism depends on leadership in Washington that consistently elucidates and educates, thus giving itself the political room it needs for maneuver abroad.

Talking It Over

A Note for Students and Discussion Groups

This issue of the HEADLINE SERIES, like its predecessors, is published for every serious reader, specialized or not, who takes an interest in the subject. Many of our readers will be in classrooms, seminars or community discussion groups. Particularly with them in mind, we present below some discussion questions—suggested as a starting point only—and references for further reading.

Discussion Questions

What are the similarities among radical regimes? the differences? Are the differences so large as to make any single policy prescription for them unrealistic?

American policy generally is based on the assumption that radical regimes pose a threat to American interests. What are those interests? How serious is this threat?

How can the American government best increase its influence with these regimes? Can the United States influence them at all? On which kinds of issues?

Why is it that the most effective American policies toward these regimes seem to have been carried out when there was the least public attention to the issue within the United States? Can pragmatic policies be presented by our public leaders in ways that will gather public support? How?

READING LIST

Destler, I.M., Gelb, Leslie H., and Lake, Anthony, *Our Own Worst Enemy: The Unmaking of American Foreign Policy*. New York, Simon & Schuster, 1984. Three men who have held high policy-making roles in the State Department and Pentagon discuss what they view as the breakdown in the making of foreign policy over the last 20 years.

Domínguez, Jorge I., and Lindenberg, Marc, "Central America: Current Crisis and Future Prospects." HEADLINE SERIES No. 271. New York, Foreign Policy Association, November/December 1984.

Feinberg, Richard E., *The Intemperate Zone: The Third World Challenge to U.S. Foreign Policy*. New York, W.W. Norton, 1983. A vice-president of the Overseas Development Council urges a neorealist approach to foreign policy.

Gutman, Roy, "Nicaragua: America's Diplomatic Charade." *Foreign Policy*, Fall 1984. Detailed history of diplomatic contacts between the United States and Nicaragua.

Hoffmann, Stanley, *Primacy or World Order*. New York, McGraw-Hill, 1980. Contains a discussion of the author's and Henry Kissinger's concepts of legitimate behavior within the international system.

"Iran-Iraq War: What Role for the U.S. in Persian Gulf?" *Great Decisions '85*. New York, Foreign Policy Association, 1985.

Karnow, Stanley, "Vietnam: The War Nobody Won." HEADLINE SERIES No. 263. New York, Foreign Policy Association, March/April 1983.

Kirkpatrick, Jeane, "Dictatorships and Double Standards." *Commentary*, November 1979. Former UN ambassador is highly critical of Carter Administration's foreign policy.

Reagan, Ronald, "America's Foreign Policy Challenges for the 1980s." *Realism, Strength, Negotiation: Key Foreign Policy Statements of the Reagan Administration*. Washington, D.C., Bureau of Public Affairs, U.S. Department of State, May 1984. April 6, 1984 address by President to Center for Strategic and International Studies, Georgetown University, Washington, D.C.

Shultz, George P., "The Future of American Foreign Policy: New Realities and New Ways of Thinking." *Department of State Bulletin*, March 1985. Secretary Shultz's statement before the Senate Foreign Relations Committee on January 31, 1985.

"South Africa and the U.S.," by the editors of the Foreign Policy Association. Twelve-page special containing background on South Africa and U.S. policy there. Summer 1985.

Vance, Cyrus, *Hard Choices: Critical Years in America's Foreign Policy*. New York, Simon & Schuster, 1983. A candid discussion of Mr. Vance's four years as head of the State Department.

A VALUABLE RESOURCE FOR TEACHERS AND STUDENTS
and a way to keep up to date on key foreign policy topics in the news . . .
Subscribe to the **HEADLINE SERIES,** published five times a year.

Each issue • is about a major world area or topic
• is written by a noted scholar
• is brief (usually 64 pages)
• is highly readable
• includes basic background, maps, charts,
discussion guides and suggested reading

- -

Titles of Past Issues on Topics of Current Interest

- -

HOW TO ORDER
Price per copy: $3.00
Quantity Discounts

19-99	25% off	500-999	35% off
100-499	30% off	1000 or more	40% off

Subscriptions

One year—$12.00
Two years—$20.00
Three years—$28.00

For information on all currently available **HEADLINE SERIES** and other FPA publications, write or call for a **free** catalog:

**Foreign Policy Association, 205 Lexington Ave., New York, NY 10016
Deloris Gruber: (212) 481-8450**